**Acknowledgements**

Illustrations by Steve Cox
Photographs by Zul Mukhida except for: pp. 8, 9, 19t Jenny
Matthews; pp. 14t Tim Garrod, 14b Jayne Knights, 15m Oliver
Cockell, 15bl Tim Richardson, 15br John Heinrich, 19b Tim
Richardson, Zul Colour Library; p. 24t Ian Harwood, 24b Nick
Hawkes, Ecoscene; p. 25b D. Parker, Tropix; p. 27 Art Directors

The author and publisher would like to thank the staff and pupils
of Balfour Infant School, Brighton.

A CIP catalogue record for this book is available
from the British Library.

ISBN 0-7136-3765-X

First published 1994 by A & C Black (Publishers) Ltd
35 Bedford Row, London WC1R 4JH

© 1994 A & C Black (Publishers) Ltd

Typeset by Rowland Phototypesetting Ltd, Bury St Edmunds, Suffolk
Printed in Belgium by Proost International Book Production

going places

# People at work

Barbara Taylor

Illustrations by Steve Cox

Photographs by Zul Mukhida and Jenny Matthews

## Contents

A & C Black · London

# What jobs do people do?

What sort of work do you do at school? Do you enjoy working or would you rather be doing something else? Does all the work you do at school count as work – even games?

How is work at home different from work at school? How many different jobs can you think of which need doing at home? Do you help with the work?

I take the register to the secretary.

I clean the paint brushes.

I tidy up the games equipment.

These children went on a work-spotting walk in their nearby town. Here are some of the tools they saw people using while they worked. Can you guess what jobs the people were doing?

(The answers are at the bottom of the page.)

What sort of jobs might the children have seen on a walk in the countryside?

# Jobs around the world

Look carefully at these photographs of people at work around the world. What sort of work are the people doing?

(The answers are at the bottom of the page.)

Do you see any of these jobs near where you live?

Vietnam

Ethiopia

2

3 El Salvador

4 El Salvador

**Answers:**

1 Cutting hair   2 Office work
3 Making shoes   4 Building homes

8

Children start doing work outside school at different ages. Are the jobs that you do different from the ones the children are doing in these pictures?

Delivering
newspapers
in Nicaragua.

Fetching water in Sri Lanka.

Collecting firewood in Mozambique.

Washing clothes in El Salvador.

# Working together

Many jobs can't be done by just one person. The work is shared out between a team of people who work together. Working together gives everybody a chance to do something they are good at. It also means that jobs are done more quickly.

Sometimes all the members of a team work in the same place and sometimes they work in different places.

1 Post workers collect the post and take it to the sorting office.

2 Here it is sorted into piles according to where it is going.

3 Then the post travels to its destination by train, lorry and aeroplane.

4 The post is delivered to our houses by postmen and women.

waiter

nurse

teacher

newspaper girl

These people all work as part of different teams.
The other members of their teams are shown below.
Can you find them?

(The answers are at the bottom of the page.)

washer-up

cook

caretaker

head teacher

doctor

newsagent

ambulance driver

reporter

**Answers:**

waiter + cook + washer-up
nurse + doctor + ambulance driver
teacher + head teacher + caretaker
newspaper girl + newsagent + reporter

11

# Why do people work?

Why do you work? Perhaps you enjoy helping people. Maybe you get paid for some of the jobs you do.

Most people need to work to earn money to provide food, clothing and shelter for themselves and their families. People also need to do important jobs that help everyone, such as collecting rubbish and driving ambulances.

I clean Mum's car to earn some extra pocket money.

Imagine what would happen if people stopped working. Look carefully at this picture. How many jobs can you see that need doing?

# When do people work?

People work at different times of the day and night. Some taxi drivers, nurses and police officers work all through the night. Bakers often start work early in the morning to bake their bread before the shops open.

Ask an adult to help you find out about when people work in your local area. Here are some of the things you could try to find out. Can you think of some other questions to ask?

Do you work during the day or at night?

Do you work at the same times each week?

How many hours do you work at a time?

You could draw work clocks like the ones here to show when different workers are at work.

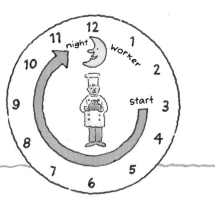

# Where people work

Some workplaces, such as hospitals and shops, need to be built in areas where people live and work. Others, such as farms and coal mines, can only be built in areas with the right climate and landscape.

Can you think of some work that only takes place in the countryside? And some work that only takes place in a town?

Many workplaces are just one step towards making something, such as a pair of jeans or a piece of paper. These workplaces need to have good links with shops, and with the places which sell the materials they need to make the goods.

Look carefully at the workplaces in these pictures. Are they in the town or in the countryside? Can you think of any reason why these workplaces are where they are?

A theatre in Japan.

A factory in Madeira.

A snack seller
on the street in India.

A gem mine in Sri Lanka.

A farm in France.

Malta airport.

Imagine you are helping to plan a new town, Alpha 10, on the planet Kriton. The people will live in homes near the landing pad.

Here is a list of work stations which need to be built in Alpha 10.

Kritonite mine

hospital

science globe

robot repair centre

food factory

Kritonite command centre

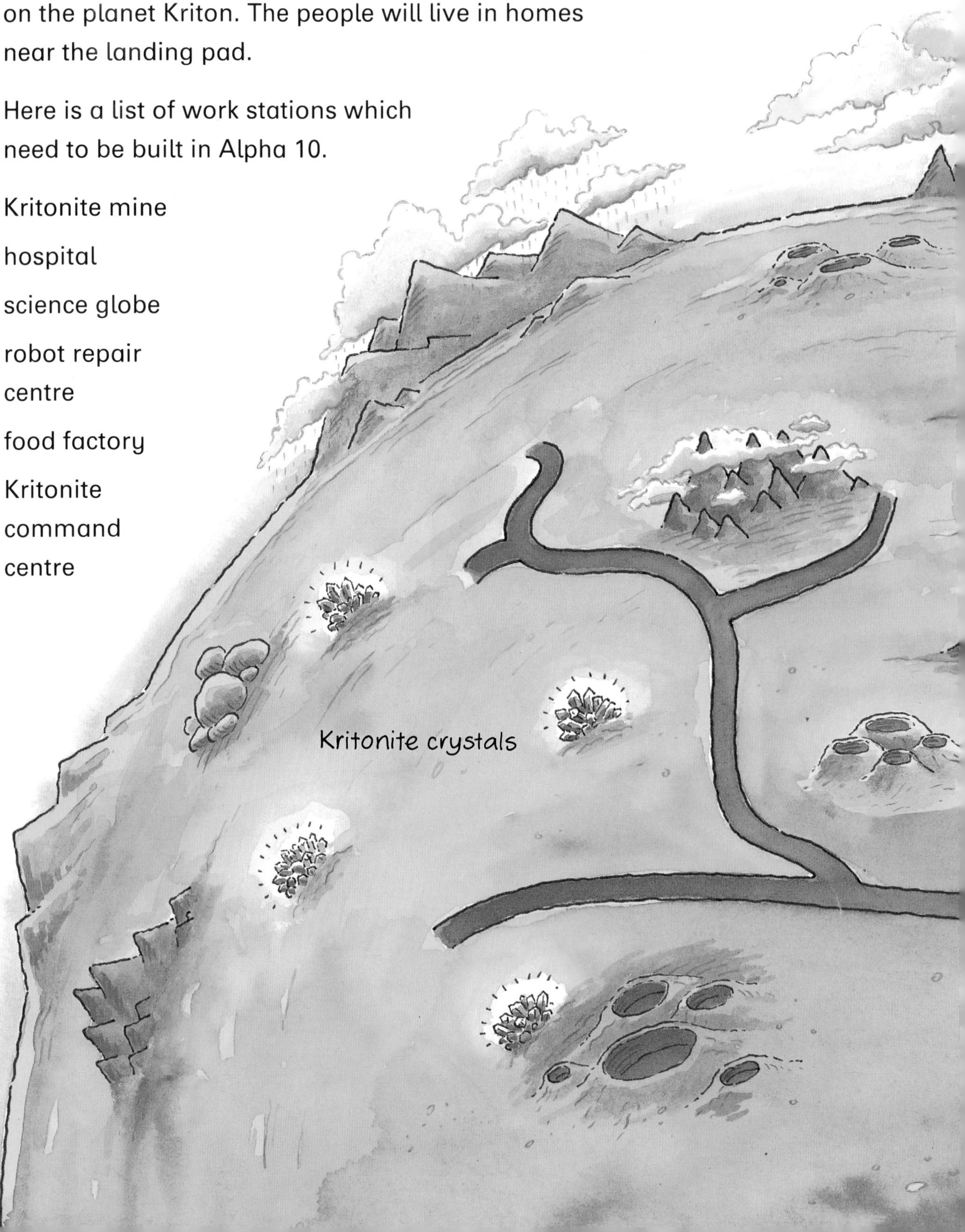

Kritonite crystals

Where is the best place to build each work station? Think about the climate, the shape of the land, where people live and where the Kritonite crystals are buried under the ground.

Draw a plan of Kriton like the one shown here. Make up symbols and draw them on your plan to show where each work station will go. Symbols are simple pictures which stand for real features such as a hospital 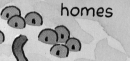 or a mine ⬡. Add a key at the side of the page to explain what the symbols mean.

homes

landing pad

homes

# Getting to work

Do you know how the teachers at your school travel to work? If they live nearby, they might walk or cycle to school. But if they live a long way away, they might travel by bus, car or train.

Applehurst

Jo lives in the village of Applehurst but has just got a job in the big city of Dinover which is twenty kilometres away.

Can you help her find the best route to work? See if you can draw a sketch of three different routes.

Dinover

# Working at home

As well as all the household jobs that people do at home, the invention of computers and other machines has made it easier for people to do other kinds of work from home.

This woman works from home as a writer.

This woman works from home as a dressmaker.

People who work at home don't have to spend time and money getting to work. They can also fit their work around other things such as leisure activities and looking after children.

# Choosing a job

What sort of work would you like to do when you are older? Here are some questions you need to think about.

What am I good at?

Do I want to work outdoors?

Do I like helping people?

Do I need to pass exams?

It's sometimes hard to decide what sort of job you want. It helps to talk to adults you know about the jobs they do. You could also ask people to come into your school and talk about their jobs, or go on a visit to a local workplace.

What sort of questions would you ask? Here are some ideas.

What job do you do?

Do you enjoy your job?

Do you work indoors or outdoors?

Do you work on your own or with other people?

How many hours do you work each day?

Did you have any special training?

How much holiday do you get?

# Finding a job

Do you know how people look for jobs? Some people find work with relatives or friends. Others reply to job advertisements in newspapers or magazines.

Have a look at some job advertisements. Think carefully about what the advertisement tells you about the job. Then see if you can make up your own job advertisement.

## Jobs

### BEES HOSPITAL
Medical Secretary

Bright, enthusiastic person wanted for busy ear, nose and throat department. Sound knowledge of medical terms needed; experience of working with the general public helpful. Must have good word-processing skills and be a non-smoker.

For more information and an application form, contact: The personnel manager, Bees Hospital, Holly Walk, Lower Marshbridge. Quote ref: 145/DC/6781
We are an equal opportunities employer.

### Polly Books
#### NATURAL HISTORY EDITOR

- Have you worked on children's information books for at least 4 years?
- Do you know a lot about animals, especially birds?
- Are you good at organising people?

If the answer to all these questions is yes, this could be the job for you.
We need an energetic and creative editor in a busy and expanding department to oversee books from the ideas stage through to finished product.

5 weeks holiday; pleasant working environment; competitive salary

Please send full cv, stating current salary to:
Caroline Marshall,
Polly Books, Birch House,
Seamoor Way, Kington.

PB

If someone wrote to you asking for a job, what sort of questions would you need to ask them to see if they were right for the job? Here are some ideas.

## Accountant
### Parktown

A building firm is looking for an accountant with solid, all round experience in a fully computerised environment. Ideal age range 30–45. Good prospects; pension scheme.

Call for interview: (3456) 78993

## SLUG CATCHER

To stop lettuces being eaten before we pick them.

Slug catching diploma, level 1 essential.

Free wellington boots with job.

Salary depends on number of slugs already caught.

Four weeks holiday.

Write with list of previous jobs, to:
Lettuce Farm, Lower Dumpling, Water-in-the-Wold, Treem

Why do you want to work here?

Which exams have you passed?

Have you done this sort of work before?

Why do you want to give up the job you are doing?

Sometimes, people find it very difficult to get a job. They might be young people who have just left school and so have no experience of work. They might be older people who have lost their job or left a job and are looking for a new one. This can be a worrying time for people who need a job to earn money for themselves and their families.

# Work and the environment

Look carefully at these two pictures. The one on the right shows an area of chalk grassland in Hampshire. The other picture shows the same area after work has started on a new piece of motorway. How has the work changed the environment?

(The answers are at the bottom of the page.)

People at work can cause a lot of damage to the environment. But there are things that we can do to help.

How could you change the work in your home or school to help the environment?

Use products made from recycled paper.

Recycle bottles and cans.

Put on an extra jumper instead of turning up the heating.

These gravel pits in Surrey have been filled with water to attract wildlife to the area.

When people finish working in an area, the damage to the environment can often be repaired. Quarries can be filled with water and used for sailing. Rubbish tips can be grassed over and planted with trees. Can you find any examples of this?

Some people have jobs taking care of the environment. Would you like a job like that?

# How jobs change

Can you find out what sort of jobs people you know did in the past? Were they the same as today? Here are some questions you could ask.

See if you can find out about the jobs done by people in your family. How have jobs changed?

What age did you start work?

How many hours a week did you work?

How did you get to work?

Did you have any training?

Mother teacher

Father reporter

Great Grandad in 1930 bus conductor

Great Grandma in 1930 shop assistant

Grandad in 1960 car mechanic

Grandma in 1960 doctor's receptionist

How you do think jobs might change in the future? Perhaps people will work shorter hours and have more time to rest and go on holiday. Robots and computers might do a lot of jobs around the home or in factories and offices.

More people will probably work from home using computers. You might even be taught by a computer or a robot at home, instead of a teacher at school. Would you like that?

# Index

# For parents and teachers
## More about the ideas in this book

*Pages 6/7* Every job has a unique set of skills. These may include the ability to make decisions, co-operate with others and help other people. Work is not always paid – school work, voluntary work, domestic chores and DIY are all unpaid.

*Pages 8/9* The type of work that people do in other parts of the world depends partly on the wealth of the country, the climate and the landscape.

*Pages 10/11* Being able to work as part of a team is an important skill to learn. Children could be encouraged to work together on a project, such as putting on a school play or making a garden.

*Page 12* Although the majority of people need to work to support themselves, a great many people also do voluntary work. Encourage the children to find out about different voluntary jobs.

*Page 13* When people work long or unsocial hours, it can affect their health and make their home life difficult.

*Pages 14/17* The location of some workplaces depends on factors such as landscape, climate, buildings, transport and wealth in an area.

*Page 18* Journeys to work can take a few minutes or several hours and can have a big impact on personal health and the environment.

*Page 19* The jobs that people do at home are as important as those in a workplace outside the home.

*Pages 20/23* Children could make a list of all the jobs which they see people doing everyday, such as a police officer or lollypop person, and make up their own job descriptions. Do men and women do the same jobs?

*Pages 24/25* A number of environmental problems are caused by work. Encourage children to find out more about the jobs people do which take care of the environment.

*Pages 26/27* Computers, robots and other machines should decrease the number of boring and heavy jobs and increase leisure time. They may also cause redundancy and unemployment.

# Things to do

**Going places** provides starting points for all kinds of cross-curricular work based on geography and the environment, both on a local and a global scale. **People at work** explores the influence of landscape and climate on the work people do and looks at working conditions, journeys to work and the impact of work on the environment. Here are some ideas for follow-up activities to extend the ideas further.

**1** Children could draw a map of an imaginary town and decide the location of various workplaces, such as factories, schools, restaurants, a radio station, shops, hospitals and bus and railways stations. They could invent symbols for each workplace and plan routes to show how people might get to different work places.

**2** One way of getting children to appreciate all the activities that go on at work and give them some experience of working together, is for them to set up their own imaginary workplace such as a library or a shop. This would give them experience of organizing people, finding resources, designing promotional material, and arranging the transportation of goods. How many different jobs are there to do? Which are the most popular? Does everybody have the same working hours?

**3** Ask the children to classify jobs into categories such as making things, building things, selling things, helping people and entertainment or leisure activities. The children could then make a list of the different qualities needed to do each type of job.

**4** Make a calendar of jobs through the year. Which jobs have to be done all year round? Which are best left for warmer weather? The jobs could be real and ordinary or weird and imaginary – perhaps on another planet.

**5** Maths activities could include making frequency tables or mapping diagrams of the most popular jobs in the classroom or home, estimating and comparing how long jobs take and calculating the time, distance and cost of different people's journeys to work.

**6** Draw a time-line of jobs in the past, the present and the future. How have the jobs changed? How have working conditions changed over the years? How have womens' jobs changed?

**7** Drama activities could be developed from the jobs in songs and stories.

**8** Visit a local workplace and make a scrapbook or a magazine about it. Children could prepare a questionnaire to find out about different jobs. During the visit, they could take photographs to record the jobs and draw a map of the workplace.

**9** Experiment with designing a machine to make a job easier, such as lifting, cleaning, writing or building something.

**10** Find out about the different animals people have trained to help them pull loads, go on journeys and assist farmers, the police and disabled people. These include dray horses, elephants, guide dogs, police dogs and horses, sheep dogs, camels and donkeys. Is it fair to make animals work for us? What about animals used for entertainment in circuses and oceanariums?

**11** Encourage the children to find out about the job of an environmental health officer. Children could take it in turns to be environmental health officers for the school. These officers could check that there is no litter in the playground, that lights are turned off in empty rooms, that paper is collected for recycling and that taps are turned off.

**12** Make a comparison between the jobs people do in your local community and the jobs people do in other parts of the country and in other countries. Are some professions local to a specific area?